WORLD'S GREATEST

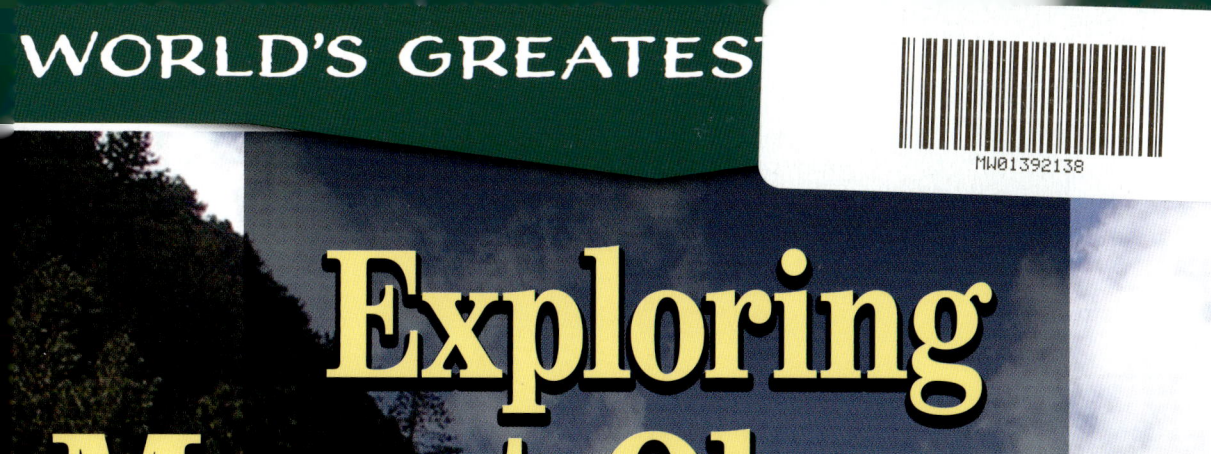

Exploring Mount Olympus

Greece's Legendary Highest Peak

Claire O'Neal

© 2024 by Curious Fox Books™, an imprint of Fox Chapel Publishing Company, Inc.

Exploring Mount Olympus is a revision, first published in 2014 by Purple Toad Publishing, Inc. Reproduction of its contents is strictly prohibited without written permission from the rights holder.

Paperback ISBN 979-8-8909-4123-7
Hardcover ISBN 979-8-8909-4124-4

The Cataloging-in-Publication Data is on file with the Library of Congress.

To learn more about the other great books from Fox Chapel Publishing, or to find a retailer near you, call toll-free 800-457-9112, send mail to 903 Square Street, Mount Joy, PA 17552, or visit us at *www.FoxChapelPublishing.com*.

We are always looking for talented authors. To submit an idea, please send a brief inquiry to acquisitions@foxchapelpublishing.com.

Fox Chapel Publishing makes every effort to use environmentally friendly paper for printing.

Printed in Malaysia

January, THURSDAY, 19. 1854.

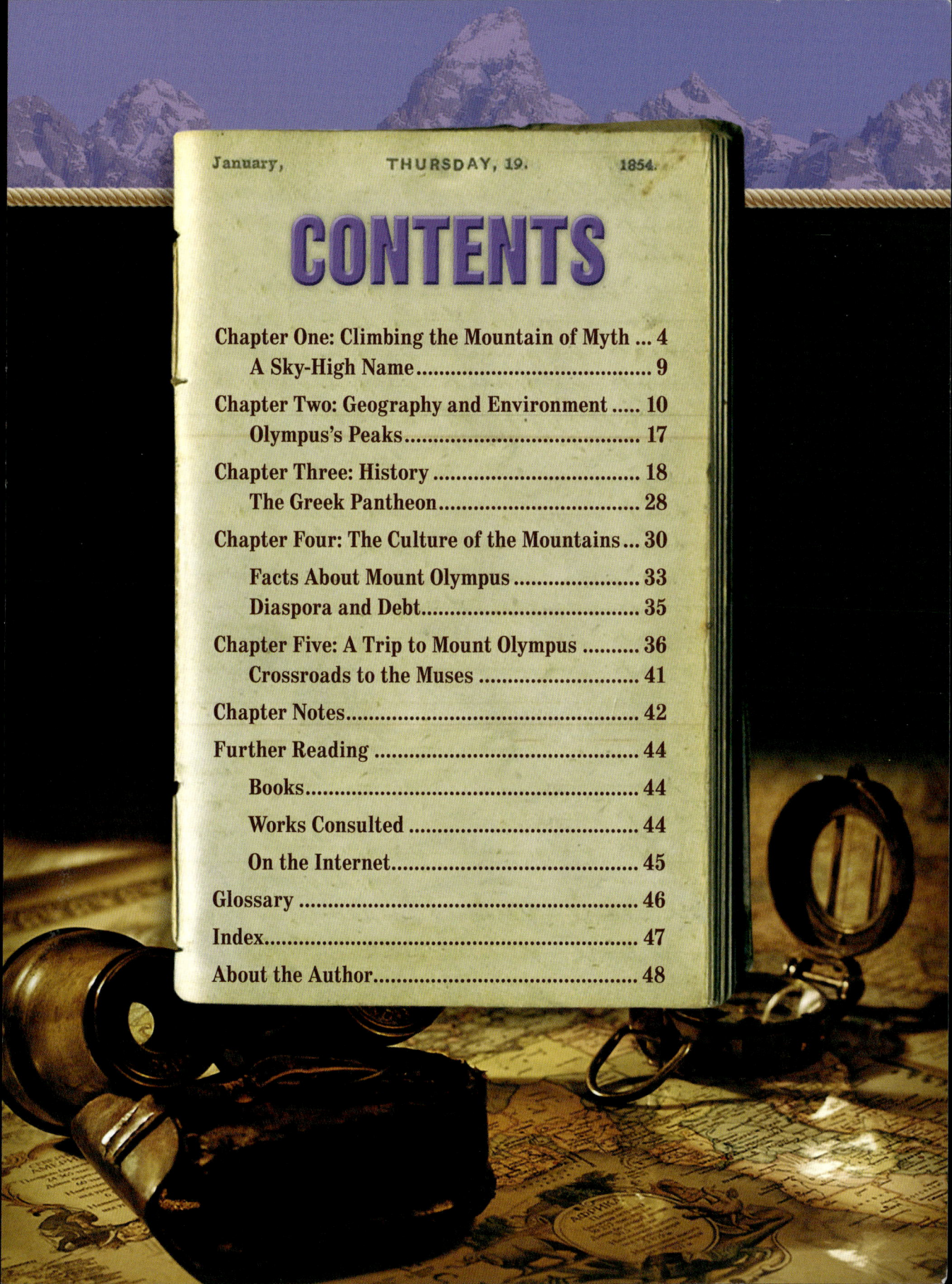

CONTENTS

Chapter One: Climbing the Mountain of Myth ... 4
    A Sky-High Name 9
Chapter Two: Geography and Environment 10
    Olympus's Peaks 17
Chapter Three: History 18
    The Greek Pantheon 28
Chapter Four: The Culture of the Mountains ... 30
    Facts About Mount Olympus 33
    Diaspora and Debt 35
Chapter Five: A Trip to Mount Olympus 36
    Crossroads to the Muses 41
Chapter Notes 42
Further Reading 44
    Books 44
    Works Consulted 44
    On the Internet 45
Glossary 46
Index 47
About the Author 48

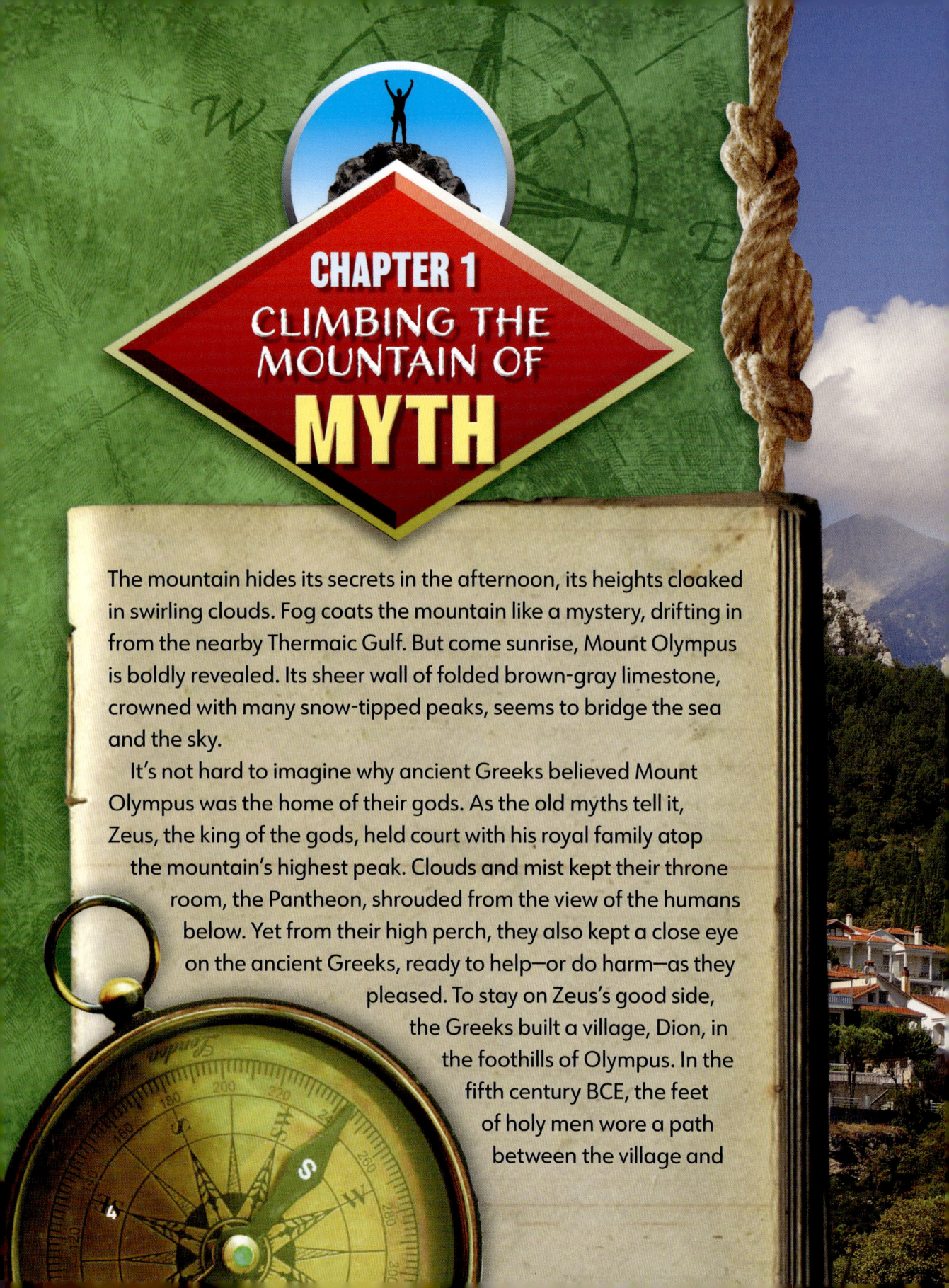

CHAPTER 1
CLIMBING THE MOUNTAIN OF MYTH

The mountain hides its secrets in the afternoon, its heights cloaked in swirling clouds. Fog coats the mountain like a mystery, drifting in from the nearby Thermaic Gulf. But come sunrise, Mount Olympus is boldly revealed. Its sheer wall of folded brown-gray limestone, crowned with many snow-tipped peaks, seems to bridge the sea and the sky.

It's not hard to imagine why ancient Greeks believed Mount Olympus was the home of their gods. As the old myths tell it, Zeus, the king of the gods, held court with his royal family atop the mountain's highest peak. Clouds and mist kept their throne room, the Pantheon, shrouded from the view of the humans below. Yet from their high perch, they also kept a close eye on the ancient Greeks, ready to help—or do harm—as they pleased. To stay on Zeus's good side, the Greeks built a village, Dion, in the foothills of Olympus. In the fifth century BCE, the feet of holy men wore a path between the village and

The village of Litochoro, tucked into the foothills of Mount Olympus.

CHAPTER 1

Ruins at the ancient sanctuaries of Dion

the foothills as they brought gifts to honor Zeus. But could mortals reach this mountain of myth? No one knows if the men of Dion dared climb to the top to meet Zeus face to face.

Legends and historical attempts are intertwined when discussing the ascent of Mount Olympus. While there are no records to confirm the attempts by figures like Sultan Mehmet IV or Edward Richter, the mountain indeed posed a significant challenge until the early twentieth century. It wasn't until August 2, 1913, that the mountain saw its first recorded summit by Christos Kakalos, along with author and art historian Daniel Baud-Bovy and photographer Frédéric Boissonnas (both of them Swiss), marking a notable moment in the history of mountaineering.

After bidding farewell to his companions, the experienced and enthusiastic Kakalos continued to explore Mount Olympus, eventually becoming the mountain's most celebrated guide. Over the years, he successfully led numerous expeditions to its various peaks, greatly contributing to the mountaineering legacy of Olympus.

In 1915, the enchanted Boissonnas published a book of breathtaking photos he had taken on his travels to Greece. His photograph *Olympus, the Pantheon* (1913) captured the magic and mystery of this famous mountain. Europeans were inspired to see it for themselves. With Kakalos as the mountain's first official guide, the tiny

Frédéric Boissonnas, 1891

CLIMBING THE MOUNTAIN OF MYTH

village of Litochoro soon hosted a steady stream of tourists looking to climb to the throne room of the gods. Rumor has it that the village was so grateful to Kakalos that the restaurant owners let him eat for free for the rest of his life.[2]

Now, ten thousand hikers climb Mount Olympus each year, drawn by its history and natural beauty. They aren't necessarily thrill-seekers or mountaineers. Though at 9,573 feet (2,918 meters), it is the highest mountain in Greece, and the second highest in the Balkan Peninsula—next to Musala in Bulgaria (9,596 feet/2,925 meters)—this mountain goes unlisted in books of the world's highest peaks. Olympus's height is nowhere near that of Asia's Mount

Olympus, the Pantheon

Everest, the world's tallest mountain at 29,035 feet (8,850 meters). Even in Europe, the loftier Alps present more technically challenging climbs, especially France's Mont Blanc, the highest peak on the continent at 15,781 feet (4,810 meters).

Instead, any reasonably fit person can hike Mount Olympus's many trails without special equipment. The main trail on Mount Olympus is a continuation of the E4, a long-distance hiking route specially designed to take outdoor enthusiasts through some of the most scenic remote areas of continental Europe. The final ascent from Skala peak to Mytikas, on the Kaka Skala ("Evil Staircase") trail, is rated Class 3 on the Yosemite Decimal Scale, a climb up a steep, exposed area that requires handholds and extra safety precautions for climbers. Though

CHAPTER 1

A runner makes his way along the main trail.

this trail does not require a rope, it is also not for the faint of heart. Its steep, natural limestone staircase is surrounded by thousand-foot drops into the fog below. Perhaps because of its popularity with inexperienced climbers, Mount Olympus has the highest accident rate among Greek mountains.[3]

Mount Olympus's visitors represent only a tiny fraction of the over thirty million tourists that visit Greece each year. These brave campers enjoy a special glimpse at the heart of Greece's history and culture, like a secret tucked away from the bustling cities and partying coasts. From the mountains came Greece's ancestors: the Mycenaeans, the Macedonians, and the Balkan peoples. From the mountains come the flavors of Greece, where rosemary, oregano, and thyme grow wild and sheep and goats climb. From the mountains comes Greece's warm and welcoming culture, a hospitality born from the need to survive. From the mountains came Greece's independence, where freedom fighters hid from the Ottoman Empire and plotted a day when their country would be free. But most famously, from the mountains came the stories of ancient Greece, myths of heroic deeds and epic betrayals that have enchanted humankind for over 3,000 years. At the heart of these stories—at the heart of all of Greece—is Mount Olympus.

A Sky-High Name

From where did the name Olympus come? Some historians suggest the word may come from prehistoric languages no longer spoken in Greece where it once meant "sky" or "power of the gods." Perhaps *Olympus* once meant "mountain," since ancient Greeks seemed to give the name to just about every mountain in sight.[4] Peaks known as "Olympus" existed in the southeastern Greece region of Attica, in the Peloponnese peninsula in Greece's southwest, on islands in the Aegean Sea, and even as far away as Turkey and the Black Sea. Many of these names persist into modern times. The Greek island of Cyprus still boasts an impressive Mount Olympus (elevation 6,404 feet/1,952 meters). But, over time, the Greeks agreed that the mythological home of their gods could only be on their country's highest mountain.

As Greece's culture spread beyond its borders, so too did the name of their most famous mountain. The United States has two Mount Olympuses, one (elevation 7,980 feet/2,432 meters) in Washington State, and one (elevation 9,030 feet/2,751 meters) in Utah. New Zealand's Mount Olympus (6,880 feet/2,096 meters) hosts a popular ski resort. And when NASA's *Mariner 9* space probe visited Mars, it sent home pictures of the largest volcano in the solar system. What name could possibly fit a mountain three times taller than Mount Everest? Of course, NASA's astronomers named it Olympus Mons.

Olympus Mons on planet Mars

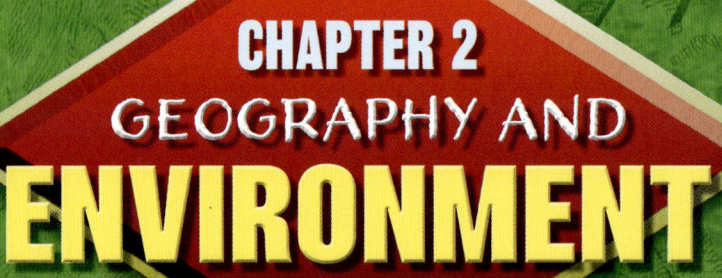

CHAPTER 2
GEOGRAPHY AND ENVIRONMENT

An old Greek joke: When God created the Earth, he took all the good soil and shook it through a sieve, sprinkling it equally over all the countries of the world. When all the soil was gone, the sieve still rattled with rocks left behind. Shrugging, God threw the rocks over his shoulder. Where they landed became the mountains and islands of Greece.

Greece is one of Europe's most mountainous countries, with hills and mountains comprising nearly 80 percent of its landscape. The mountain ranges were primarily formed between 45 and 20 million years ago, during significant tectonic activities when the African tectonic plate collided with the Eurasian Plate. This collision helped shape not only Greece's mountainous terrain but also influenced other mountainous regions across Mediterranean Europe, including the Alps and the Pyrenees. The African Plate continues to move toward the Eurasian Plate at an average rate of about an inch each

The 600-year-old Holy Trinity Monastery perches atop a 1,300-foot (400-meter) rock tower in Meteora.

CHAPTER 2

year, contributing to ongoing geological dynamics in the region. Even this tiny motion slowly, steadily crunches rock and lifts Greece's mountains ever higher. The tiny plate motion also produces the earthquakes that rock Greece on a regular basis. One struck Athens in 1999, killing 143 people and injuring over 1,000. When a large earthquake shook the Aegean Sea on July 9, 1956, it generated a tsunami that threatened the entire region.[1]

Most of Greece's lofty peaks belong to the Pindus Range, Greece's major mountain chain. Sometimes known as Greece's spine, the Pindus Mountains run

Topography of Greece, Turkey, and the Baltic Peninsula

GEOGRAPHY AND ENVIRONMENT

parallel to Greece's western coastline from its northern borders with the countries of Albania and Macedonia, south to Greece's Peloponnese peninsula. The same mountain range even continues out to sea, its peaks poking out of the water to make many of the Aegean Islands.

Mount Olympus is located in northeastern Greece and is part of the Olympus Range. The mountain itself rises as a high ridge, tipped with 52 peaks, taking up an area of nearly 200 square miles (500 square kilometers) between the boundary between the Greek regions of Thessaly and Central Macedonia. Its northern side, facing Central Macedonia, is its most severe, with steep slopes that separate sharp ridges from deep canyons. Clouds that gather over the north face create twelve times as many thunderstorms as anywhere else in Greece. In ancient times, this stormy nature surely fed the mountain's reputation as Zeus's throne room.[2] The eastern face's gentler slopes, weathered by many small streams, make it the more popular choice for hiking trails. Because the coast of the Thermaic Gulf lies at sea level less than 10 miles (16 kilometers) away, Mount Olympus's foothills are very low, giving the mountain a very large prominence—one of the largest in Europe. They make the mountain seem taller than it actually is.

The weather in Greece's mountains seems wild and extreme compared to the predictable, mild weather of the more densely populated coasts. Thanks to their Mediterranean climate, Greece's coasts experience over 250 sunny days every year. Hot, dry summers in these lowlands give way to a handful of cool, wet days in winter. Greece's mountains take the sea air and chill it, squeezing out its moisture as fog, rain, or snow. Though Greece is too sunny for true glaciers to form, peaks higher than 6,500 feet (1,982 meters) keep their snow-dusted tops from September until the end of May. Mount Olympus itself can receive over 22 feet (7 meters) of snow in the winter.[3] On occasional years, its highest peak, Mytikas, can remain snow-covered year-round, but much of the mountain's snow pack melts in July and August.

Greece's mountains provide important resources—and jobs—to the country.

CHAPTER 2

The enormous heat and pressure of mountain building turns earth materials into rich and useful resources. From the iron deposits throughout Greece came the metal that made ancient life possible, with pots and pans, plows, and swords. Philip II of ancient Macedon became fabulously wealthy from gold mines of northern Greece.[4] Marble quarries near Mount Olympus produced Verde Antico, the bleached white stone with gray and green veins that continues to be prized throughout the world. Today, Greece is a global leader in producing huntite and perlite. Huntite is a special mineral that helps make plastics safer by making them less flammable. Perlite is a type of volcanic glass that, when heated, expands and is used to insulate homes and make ceiling tiles lighter and more efficient. Greece also mines important materials like nickel and bauxite, and although it has historically been a major producer of lignite, a type of coal, the country is shifting towards greener energy sources.

Greece's mountainous center and north are also home to nearly all of the country's remaining forests. Though forests originally covered much of Greece, thousands of years of use by humans—and goats—have changed the landscape. Most of Greece is now dominated by towns and tourist areas. Dictator Ioannis Metaxas (1871–1941, ruled 1936–1941) established Mount Olympus and the forest on its flanks as Greece's first national park in 1938, creating a preserve that protects the plants and animals there.

Take Mount Olympus's high elevation, mix it with its nearness to the Thermaic Gulf, and you get a unique ecological setting. From its base to its peak, Mount Olympus's slopes experience each of the four vegetation zones possible in mainland Europe. Twenty-five percent of all of Greece's plants are accounted for in the more than 1,700 species that live on Mount Olympus. Some of these are protected species, rare and important to Greece and the Balkans. Because more than 130 of these plant species are so important to Greece's conservation efforts, the United Nations Educational, Scientific, and Cultural Organization (UNESCO) declared Mount Olympus an International Biosphere Reserve in 1981.[5]

Lower elevations (up to 1,640 feet, or 500 meters) on Mount Olympus

GEOGRAPHY AND ENVIRONMENT

The wildflower meadows of Mount Olympus attract many species of colorful butterflies. The ancient Greeks called them psyche, which means "soul."

experience weather typical of a Mediterranean climate—hot and dry summers with cooler, wet winters. Most of Olympus's plant species live in this zone. Here, the dense brush of low trees and shrubs makes up the *maquis*, an Italian word meaning "thicket." Maquis plants grow out of the dry soil or even rock that covers much of Greece. Trees and shrubs such as holm oak, the Greek strawberry tree, cedar trees, the Judas tree, and the turpentine tree have leathery leaves that protect their moisture from Greece's hot sun. Herbs like sage, juniper, oregano, and bay perfume the maquis and lend their flavors to Greek villagers' home-cooked dishes. Many maquis plants, such as gorse, tree heath, poppies, and rhododendron, produce a riot of wildflowers that color Olympus's meadows between April and July. They also attract rainbow crowds of butterflies, one of Olympus's claims to fame.

Dense montane forests make up the second zone (up to 4,600 feet, or 1,400 meters). Species common to forests in the mountains of central Europe, such as black pine, Greek fir, European beech, wych elm, cherry, and hazel trees, create a shaded canopy where mossy plants carpet the forest floor. Here, Olympus's wrinkled rock creates many ravines, gullies, and waterfalls. Bulbs such as irises, crocuses, and tulips color the shade near the streams, where water-loving trees

CHAPTER 2

Syrian woodpecker of Greece

like grey willow, alder, and oriental plane grow. Reptiles and amphibians, including the fire salamander, seek out this wet and protected environment. Over one hundred species of birds nest in these forests and on the mountain slopes, such as woodpeckers, bee-eaters, and the threatened golden eagle. Thanks to its location between Europe, Africa, and Asia, Mount Olympus serves as an important crossroads for many species of migratory birds.

Hardy conifers thrive in the third zone (up to 8,200 feet, or 2,500 meters). Moisture from the Thermaic Gulf condenses in the cooler air at these higher elevations, creating rain and snow as well as Olympus's mysterious fog. Species native to the Balkan Peninsula take over here, including European beech and Bosnian pine, along with shrubs and grass plants. Olympus's stands of Bosnian pine grow at elevations as high as 8,200 feet (2,500 meters), forming the highest mountain forest in the Balkans. Animals flock to its cool shade. The gray-brown roe deer, wild boar, beech marten, red squirrel, red fox, golden jackal, and gray wolf all live in this zone. The threatened Balkan chamois, an antelope-like wild goat, struggles to survive here, a victim of illegal modern-day hunting. Brown bears once roamed Olympus's slopes, as well. Sadly, the last bear on Mount Olympus died in 2008. Today, bears are seen only rarely, their range shrunk to the northern Pindus Mountains.

The tree line stops at the alpine zone above 8,200 feet (2,500 meters). Snow cover from September to May prevents many plants from growing. Hardy dwarf shrubs do survive from year to year. Herbaceous plants, including native Greek wildflowers, explode with growth in the spring and summer, only to be killed by fall's frost each year. Particularly famous is the *Jankaea heldreichii,* a lavender-flowering African violet found nowhere else in the world, whose silvery green foliage springs out of Olympus's limestone crags.

Olympus's Peaks

Mount Olympus rises as a stark, high ridge, tipped with many peaks. The Olympic National Park counts 52 in all. The top ten highest are:

Mytikas (or Ktenia; or Zeus's Throne)—9,573 feet/2,918 meters
Skolio—9,548 feet/2,911 meters
Stefani—9,542 feet/2,909 meters
Skala—9,400 feet/2,866 meters
Agios Antonios—9,235 feet/2,815 meters
Profitis Ilias—9,196 feet/2,803 meters
Megali Toumba—9,190 feet/2,801 meters
Mikri Toumba—8,990 feet/2,740 meters
Christaki—8,878 feet/2,706 meters
Kalogeros—8,862 feet/2,701 meters

Mytikas

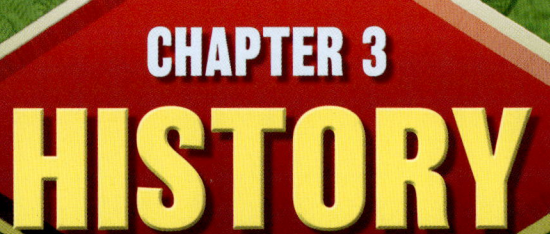

CHAPTER 3
HISTORY

Greece's location at the crossroads of Europe, Asia, and Africa has attracted settlers since the dawn of time. Hunter-gatherer tribes of prehistoric humans became some of the original "cavemen" in the mountains of northern Greece. Human ancestors, like the Neanderthals, sought shelter in the mountains' caves as early as 240,000 years ago.[1] Civilization arrived from Crete and present-day Turkey around 7000 BCE. Those settlers brought farming with them, introducing Greece to food crops such as barley, vegetables, and olives. They also introduced tamed goats and sheep. These surefooted animals thrived on the rocky hills of Greece. Even today, their milk and meat continue to be an important part of nearly every Greek's diet.

Around 2600 BCE, Greece's first great civilization began to spread along the Mediterranean Sea. The Minoan people built a vast seagoing trading empire, taking precious metals

The mountains of Greece provided early civilizations with shelter. Its location on the sea allowed trade, bringing prosperity.

CHAPTER 3

Bull Leapers, *fresco from the Palace of Knossos, Crete*

such as tin, copper, gold, and silver to markets as far away as Egypt or Spain. Because of their great wealth, Minoans enjoyed luxuries such as games, art, and even education. Children and adults alike played sports, especially boxing and bull leaping. Minoan women priests worshiped deities in their temples. Minoan painters created stunning works of art, including colorful frescoes, or wall paintings, in their temples and palaces. The ancient Minoans, possibly influenced by earlier civilizations like the Egyptians, developed their own unique script known as Linear A. This writing system was used extensively on clay tablets to manage and document economic transactions and administrative details. Many of these tablets, along with vibrant frescoes, have been discovered in the Minoan capital of Knossos on the island of Crete. These artifacts offer archaeologists valuable insights into the rich, complex society that flourished in ancient Crete. No one knows why the civilization mysteriously collapsed around 1500 BCE.

HISTORY

The war-loving Mycenaean civilization to the north seized its chance to conquer Minoan territory. Between 1600 BCE and 1100 BCE, the kingdom of Mycenae expanded from its original capital, on the Peloponnese peninsula in southwestern Greece, to control Mediterranean islands in the south, the mountains of Epirus and Macedonia in the north, and everything between. Archaeologists have dug up temples and even a cemetery near Mount Olympus that dates to this time period. The mountain may have been a holy place to these ancient peoples. Though the Mycenaean civilization faded around 1100 BCE, stories of their deeds lived on. The heroic battles they fought against their enemies in Troy later inspired the famous poems of Homer, *The Iliad* and *The Odyssey,* which were written around 750 BCE.

Over the next three centuries, the city-state style of government arose in Greece. As Greeks naturally settled in the valleys between the country's many hills and mountains, the landscape blocked cities off from each other. With no lord or king to unite them, Greece's largest communities got used to operating independently. Hundreds of the largest cities, including Athens, Sparta, and

The Acropolis of Athens, Greece

CHAPTER 3

Corinth, made their own laws, chose their own leaders, and led their own armies. Most Greek city-states were located along the coasts of Greece, Italy, or present-day Turkey. The sea gave them easy access to trade routes, as well as a pleasant climate nearly year-round. By around 800 BCE, city-states had spread as far north as the plains of Thessaly.

Meanwhile, on the north side of Olympus, the kingdom of Macedon gained territory and importance. Originally based in Greece's mountainous northeast, Macedonians pushed south, over Mount Olympus, to expand their territory into parts of Thessaly in the seventh century BCE. Macedon operated like a typical ancient civilization, ruled by a king with huge armies and the means to use them, but its culture intertwined with that of Greece. Macedonians spoke and wrote in ancient Greek, and they worshiped the same gods. Mount Olympus held a special place in their hearts, and in its northeastern foothills they built a sacred village to honor Zeus, the king of their gods. *Dion* (taken from dios, which was Greek for "Zeus" or "god") became the site of lavish festivals. There, Macedonian King Archelaos I (reigned 413–399 BCE) hosted theater and athletic competitions to honor Zeus and his daughters, the Muses.

Though some Greek city-states were practically next door to Macedon, the glow of ancient Greece's Golden Age did not shine on Macedon. The artists and intellectuals of Athens built the foundations of math and science. They used them to construct awe-inspiring buildings such as the Parthenon. The warriors of Sparta in the Peloponnese trained constantly for battle against enemy city-states. To both, faraway Macedonia was out of sight, out of mind.

However, the hearts of all ancient Greeks lay with Mount Olympus, nestled in Macedonian territory at the northern end of Thessaly's plain. The Greeks believed that the gods and goddesses who controlled their world kept a throne room on Mount Olympus. These gods were not holy and untouchable idols. Greek gods had the same hopes and problems as normal mortals did—They got married and had kids! They argued with their family! They fought one another!—but they never aged and never died. Like superheroes, they had strengths and

HISTORY

Alexander the Great was an involved, active ruler. This eighteenth-century painting shows him giving instructions to an architect as they build the city of Alexandria together.

weaknesses that set them up for trouble. Greek poets Homer and Hesiod gave the gods starring roles in their stories of Greece's history, stories the Greeks loved to tell again and again.

Unfortunately, the Greek city-states spent more time fighting one another than they did telling stories. After Athens and Sparta destroyed each other in the Peloponnesian Wars (which ended in 404 BCE), Macedon swept south and took control. Their ruler, King Philip II (382–336 BCE), allowed the city-states to keep their culture and government, but encouraged them to work together in an association called the League of Corinth. Phillip's son, Alexander III (356–323

CHAPTER 3

Constantine was proclaimed Emperor in 306 CE at a Roman fortress in York, England, a few feet away from where this statue was placed.

BCE), led the League of Corinth to victory against everyone in the known world. Alexander the Great, as he became known, expanded his kingdom from his homeland of Greece to as far south as Egypt and as far east as India in less than thirteen years. When he died from an illness at only thirty-two years old, his overstretched kingdom was doomed to collapse.

The rising Roman Empire claimed Greece by 148 BCE, and would hold most of the Balkan Peninsula for the next 500 years. The Romans admired Greek culture and language and adopted many of its customs. Roman nobles sent their children to school in Athens, considered a world-leading center of learning and culture. At first, Romans worshipped the gods of Greece, though they gave them different names. But when Emperor Constantine converted to Christianity in 313 CE, he forced the entire empire to share his religion. Constantine also rebuilt the city of Byzantium in present-day Turkey to create a second capital, Constantinople, which would become the seat of his Eastern Roman Empire. The ever-faithful Constantine declared Koine Greek the new official language. Though Rome fell in the fifth century CE, the Byzantine Empire persisted halfway through the fifteenth century, with Greece under its control.

Unfortunately for the Greeks, their faraway rulers could not protect them against the Germanic tribes laying waste to Europe. Greece was overrun by

HISTORY

tribes of Visigoths in the fourth century. When the Visigoths fell, Slavic tribes controlled most of the Balkan Peninsula between the sixth and eighth centuries, eventually settling in north and northeastern Greece. They were joined by the Vlach clans, sheep and goat herders from the mountains of central and eastern Europe. Though these tribes brought destruction and death, today's Greek population, especially in the north, counts them as their ancestors.

To protect their religion and themselves, the monks of Greece took to the hills in the most spectacular way. In 963, Athanasius the Athonite (c. 920–1003) dedicated a monastery on the secluded Mount Athos. No females have been allowed on the mountain—not even female animals—since 1046. Other monks snuck away to the Pindus Range. Beginning in the fourteenth century, they built stone monasteries atop dizzying sandstone spires in the Meteora Range of northern Greece. These postcard-perfect castles and forts are today famous tourist attractions.

In the fifteenth century, the Byzantine Empire crumbled against the armies of the Ottoman Empire from the Middle East and North Africa. Greece came under Ottoman control by 1456. The Ottomans were tolerant rulers who allowed their conquered people to keep their local customs, religion, and language, as long as these did not interfere with their ability to pay taxes. The Greeks were not so tolerant. They viewed the Ottomans as godless heathens because their Islamic religion revered Allah and the Prophet Muhammad instead of Rome's God and Jesus Christ. Greeks especially took offense when their Ottoman rulers allowed Jewish exiles from Spain to settle in Thessaloniki in 1492.[2] Though they grumbled, the unorganized Greeks knew they stood no chance against the powerful and well-armed Ottomans. Even so, bands of freedom fighters hid in mountain caves known only to locals, plotting and sometimes striking out at Ottoman forces.

Rigas Feraios (1757–1798), a native son of Thessaly, gave voice and inspiration to Greeks who wished the Ottomans gone.[3] Inspired by the French Revolution, Feraios in turn inspired his Greek and Balkan countrymen to rise up against the

CHAPTER 3

Ottomans. He and his band of rebels hid out in the caves of Mount Olympus, encouraging locals to fight against "the Turkish tyrant's yoke."[4] He wrote a *thourios ymnos,* or war hymn, and drafted a constitution and the first map of modern Greece. In the 1820s, Feraios's efforts caught the attention of Hellenophiles—lovers of ancient Greek language and culture—in the universities of mainland Europe. Scholars in Great Britain, France, and Russia persuaded their countries to support Greece's fight for independence. Some intellectuals traveled to Greece to join the battle, including famous British poet Lord Byron. Backed by such powerful friends, Greece declared war on the Ottomans in 1821. With much help from the powers of Europe, Greece arose victorious in 1832.

Legend says Greece's revolution was declared when Bishop Germanos blessed the rebel's banner on March 25, 1821. The banner would later become Greece's national flag.

HISTORY

The rocky Dodecanese islands have a rich history. Though small, many islands boast historic churches and castles.

At first, the Kingdom of Greece held only a fraction of its land today—the southern mainland, the Peloponnese, and a few Aegean Islands. The new country slowly added territory, fueled by the Megali Idea (literally, "Big Idea") that Greece should grow to house all Greek people. Greece gained Mount Olympus and Thessaly from the Ottomans in 1881, and Epirus and Macedonia after the Balkan Wars of 1913.[5] Greece lost ground during World War II. Despite dictator Ioannis Metaxas's loud *"Ohi!"* (No!), the Axis Powers of Bulgaria, Italy, and Germany occupied Greece and much of the Balkan Peninsula. But with Italy's defeat, Greece gained the Dodecanese islands in 1947, completing Greece's modern borders. The government of Greece spent the next few years in a tumult of kings and dictators. In 1974, the country rewrote its constitution to return the government to a free democracy, the ideas of which were first formed in ancient Athens.

The Greek Pantheon

Homer paints a vivid portrait of the ancient Greek gods and goddesses, but ideas for these immortal figures had been around for a thousand years before him, since the time of the Minoans and Mycenaeans. After ancient Greece fell, Romans continued their worship for 500 years. Here are the most famous of the Olympians—the deities who lived on Olympus—listed with their Greek and Roman names.

Zeus/Jupiter: King of the gods and god of the sky, Zeus rose from being a minor god in Minoan religion to the highest place in Greek myth. Zeus had a quick temper; he threw lightning bolts and yelled thunder at his haughty goddess wife, Hera.

Hera/Juno: Queen of the Gods, goddess of marriage. Once powerful and beloved as the Minoan Great Goddess, Hera became a jealous and angry wife in Greek myth.

Hades/Pluto: God of the underworld (where souls existed after death), brother of Zeus. While Hades ruled the underworld, he was not the god of death.

Poseidon/Neptune: God of the sea and earthquakes, brother of Zeus. Many ancient Greek cities chose him as their protector.

Aphrodite/Venus: Goddess of love and beauty. She arose fully formed from the sea.

Athena/Minerva: Goddess of wisdom and war. In myths, great men often owed their success to having her as their ally.

Demeter/Ceres: Goddess of the harvest and seasons. When her daughter, Persephone/Proserpina, was stolen away by Hades, god of the underworld, Demeter's sadness created winter.

Hermes/Mercury: Messenger god. This quick-witted protector of travelers helped mortals travel to the afterlife.

Hephaestus/Vulcan: God of fire and blacksmithing. His Roman name is the source of the word *volcano.*

Apollo/Apollo: God of the sun, music, and poetry. Greeks asked for Apollo's help in times of sickness, and his wisdom at the famous Oracle of Delphi.

Artemis/Diana: Goddess of the hunt. Artemis had many roles, including protecting forests, wildlife, and women in childbirth.

Ares/Mars: God of war. This bloodthirsty god starred in epic poems of battle, but was not popular among Greek worshippers.

Hestia/Vesta: Goddess of the home and family. Greek families offered their first household sacrifice to her.

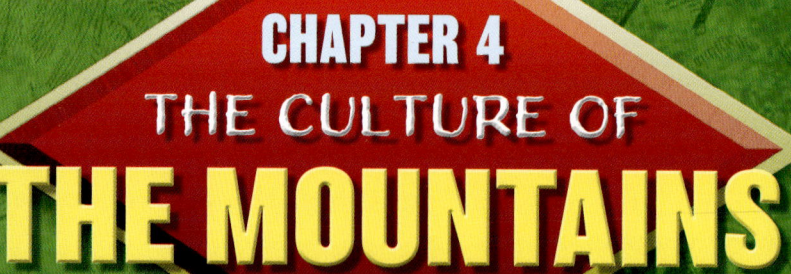

CHAPTER 4
THE CULTURE OF THE MOUNTAINS

In this ancient land, time has helped the people of Greece choose which old-world traditions are worth keeping alive in their modern country. Ruins remain amid skyscrapers in Athens. Mountain villagers chat on cell phones as they herd their goats using traditional methods. Where past generations of Greeks matched their strength in battle games or war, today's Greeks throw their energy into other battles. They haggle for the best prices with vendors at the village market or rail at the TV as they cheer for their national soccer team. Interestingly, this long-lived culture also produces long-lived people. Today, the life expectancy of the average Greek is 79 years for men and 84 years for women, higher than that of the United States.[1] Medical studies point to the health benefits of the Greek diet, with lots of fresh fruit, vegetables, fish, olive oil, yogurt, and red wine. But perhaps most important to their longevity is the passion Greeks share for family, community, and history.

Athens, as seen from the ancient Agora, or marketplace

CHAPTER 4

Greeks are world-famous for their outgoing personalities and hospitality. Before modern times, this welcoming attitude served as a defense against starvation. Between the rocky, harsh soil of the mountains and the drought-prone coasts, whole years of crops could wither and die. Greeks banded together, forming tight-knit communities that shared food and resources. They also considered it their sacred duty to help travelers, for whom a hunk of bread and feta cheese could mean the difference between life and death. Even today, *xenos,* the Greek word for "stranger," also means "houseguest."

The Greek language links today's Greece to its past. It has been continuously written and spoken in one way or another since Linear A arose in 1500 BCE.[2] By 2012, around 13 million people worldwide were speaking the Greek language. However, language does change with the times. Everyday Greek citizens no longer speak scholarly Koine Greek or Katharevousa, the language of the Greek Church. In 1976, Greek law declared Demotic Greek, a related but modern dialect, the official written and spoken language. Whether urging a midfielder to kick the goal already, reciting ancient poetry, or singing an Ottoman-era love song, Greeks everywhere pride themselves in speaking their native tongue.

The Greek Orthodox Christian Church dominates nearly every aspect of life in Greece. It is the official state religion, written into Greece's constitution, and practiced by 98 percent of Greek citizens. Both government and society live according to the church calendar. The Greek government even pays for church maintenance and for the salaries of the Orthodox priests. Orthodox churches are in every village, no matter how small, their rounded domes blending with the hilly landscape. Muslims settled in the mountainous northeast during the Ottoman Empire and today make up the largest religious minority, at less than 2 percent of the population. A tiny following of Greek pagans—estimates range from 2,000 to 100,000 followers—worship the ancient Greek gods. Once outlawed by the Roman Emperor Theodosius in the 4th century CE, the Greek government officially recognized this religion in 2006.[3]

Part of what makes religion so special for Greeks is their love of community

Facts About Mount Olympus

Name: Mount Olympus. Also spelled Olympos or Olimbos

Height: 9,573 feet (2,918 meters) at peak Mytikas (meaning "nose")

Prominence: 7,726 feet (2,355 meters)

Origin of name: unknown

GPS coordinates: 40.0834° N, 22.3499° E

Country: Greece

Range: Olympus

Location: On the border between the Regions of Thessaly and Central Macedonia. According to the Greek government, Mount Olympus is located in Dio-Olympos, the southernmost municipality of Pieria, which is the southernmost regional unit of the Greek Region of Central Macedonia.

Closest village: Litochoro (pop. 7,000)

Nearest major cities:

Katerini (pop. 82,892), 24 miles/39 kilometers;

Larissa (pop. 268,963), 52 miles/85 kilometers;

Thessaloniki (pop. 814,980), 67 miles/108 kilometers

Time zone: Eastern Europe

First recorded summit: August 2, 1913, by Christos Kakalos (Greece) with Daniel Baud-Bovy and Frederic Boissonnas (Switzerland)

Climbing difficulty: Moderate hike. Kakoskala, the trail from Skala peak to the Mytikas summit, is rated Class 3 on the Yosemite Decimal Scale.

Fastest climbing time: 5 hours, 19 minutes, 45 seconds by Kilian Jornet (Spain) on June 10, 2011

CHAPTER 4

Greeks going to their village church during a panigyri.

celebrations. A *panigyri*—a feast day for a religious reason—can be as huge as Easter or Christmas or as small as the birthday of a village's patron saint. After solemn church services, shop owners and locals set up tables in the town square where everyone can dine on fresh fruits and vegetables, mouthwatering roasted lamb, and bottles of wine. Music from singers and the bouzouki, a Greek lute, fills the air with folk songs that celebrate life, love, and friends into the wee morning hours. Friends and family alike join in traditional Greek dances. A male leader playfully waves a handkerchief in the *kalamatianos* circle dance. The rousing *tsamikos* dance mimics a battle, with stomping, jumping, and rousing shouts of "*opa!*" In the summer, *panigyri* gatherings can swell to include almost everyone in the village, as neighbors near and far come together to enjoy the festivities. This vibrant celebration of community and culture showcases the deep connections and joyful spirit that characterize traditional Greek social life.

Diaspora and Debt

Eking a living out of the Greek landscape has always been unpredictable. If the going got too rough, parents encouraged their grown children to move far away, even to another country, to make a living. Once settled, the emigrant children sent money back to Greece to support the family. Though aid from the European Union prevents modern Greeks from starving, this practice continues today. As many as 6 million Greeks work abroad, a population known as the diaspora.[4] By 2012, Greece's failing economy was making the diaspora more important than ever. Though business in the country had been slow since 2007, the Greek government took the country to financial ruin, creating the Greek Debt Crisis of 2009. As of 2024, Greece has an unemployment rate of about 10%. Although Greece remains high on the world's debt list, it has seen major improvement over the past 15 years. In recent years, tourism has increased, causing Greece's economy to steadily increase. In summer of 2023, over 10 million people visited Greece, bringing in over 21 billion euros of revenue. This, along with other strategic decisions by Greece's government, has given Greeks high hopes for their economic future.

People in Thessaloniki crowd around a truck to buy sacks of potatoes. In northern Greece, farmers save money for themselves and their customers by bringing their produce directly to the people.

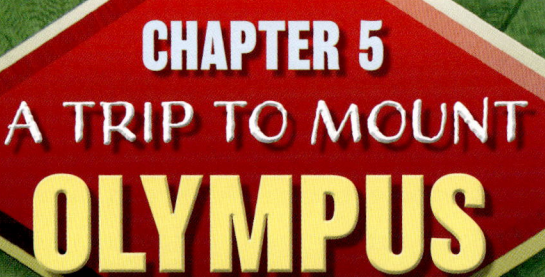

CHAPTER 5
A TRIP TO MOUNT OLYMPUS

Visitors from Europe and abroad mostly come to walk among the ancient architecture of Athens, or to relax on Greece's sun-drenched coast. Few tourists visit the mountains, though they lie at the edge of every view. With their welcoming villages and unspoiled nature, these mountains offer plenty of entertainment. For hiking buffs and history fans alike, Mount Olympus is the rarest find of all—the famous throne room of ancient Greek gods is also a world-class nature preserve.

Mount Olympus comes into view on the drive from Athens to Thessaloniki, towering over the flat plain of Thessaly. Off the coastal highway lies the small village of Litochoro, tucked away in Olympus's foothills. From there Olympus looms large, wrinkled and exposed. A winding, 11 miles (18 kilometers) road leads from the edge of Litochoro to Olympus National Park. Many hikers drive this way to get to the trail's beginning. Others take the four-hour walk

Olympus National Park protects about 10,000 acres of land, a home to unique plants and wildlife.

37

CHAPTER 5

from Litochoro along the Enipeas Gorge.[1] The path dances over the babbling Enipeas River on wooden bridges. Streams cascade down the mountain's weathered, broken faces of limestone, watering mossy rock gardens below. Just before the major trailhead lies a stone monastery, built by St. Dionysios in the fifteenth century. Much of the building was left in ruins after the Germans bombed it during World War II. The Nazis suspected that Greek rebels hid inside (and they were right). Now, a small number of monks still call it home. They welcome tourists to take a look, pray, or even spend the night.

The road ends at Prionia, where a red-roofed log cabin serves as both a restaurant and the start of the most popular trail up the mountain. Nearly all of Greece basks in the hot sun, but here, a blanket of shade invites travelers to stretch their legs. The trail upward follows natural steps in broken stone. Before long, the forest trees shorten to stumpier ones that can handle the harsh, long winter. Over the scrub, sweeping views of the lush green mountain, the Thermaic Gulf, and the bright blue sky dazzle. Unlike Athens, which lives under a blanket of smog, the air here is clean and pure.

Olympus has eight refuges—on-trail hotels—that invite hikers to spend a comfortable night on the mountain. Though a fit person can hike from Prionia to Mytikas and back again in a long day, summiting over the course of two days is a better idea. Because the peak of Mount Olympus has less oxygen compared to the coastal foothills, hiking too fast is extra tiring, and aching muscles may threaten to call it quits at dangerous times. Another important perk to an overnight stay: by reaching the highest ground the next morning, hikers can enjoy the views without the fog that often rolls in from the Thermaic Gulf in the afternoon.

The most popular refuge, Spilios Agapitos, also known as Refuge A, waits at 6,890 feet (2,100 meters) up, tucked into the forest atop a natural limestone shelf. Refuge A stays open from May to October and can sleep up to 110 guests.[2] The refuge offers luxuries uncommon to average trails. Visitors ease their weary feet out of hiking boots at the door, slipping into sandals provided

A TRIP TO MOUNT OLYMPUS

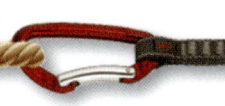

Spilios Agapitos

by the refuge's hosts. Instead of a tasteless camp dinner of granola bars, Spilios Agapitos refuels hikers' bellies and spirits with a homemade dinner of simple Greek classics like bean soup, pasta, fresh bread and cheese, and tea made with herbs plucked from the mountain. Diners share rustic wooden tables with hikers from around the world. Instead of a cold night spent tossing and turning in a sleeping bag on the rocky ground, the refuge tucks sleepers into clean bunk beds with thick, soft blankets. In the morning, a simple, traditional Greek breakfast of fresh-baked bread with jam and honey and homemade feta cheese prepares visitors for the three-hour hike ahead.

After the first thirty minutes beyond the refuge, hikers are higher than trees can grow. Suddenly, the forest drops away and the bare ridge is surrounded by peaks. The path becomes steeper, and loose rocks make ankle-tight hiking boots a necessity. On one side, the ground simply falls away into the thin mountain air. On the other, The Cauldron waits below. This rocky bowl is nearly always swathed in fog. On good days, Olympus's many peaks bare their ancient, wrinkled rock in dappled sunlight. But on bad ones, the climb can become dangerous, even deadly. Fierce wind gusts of 30 to 50 miles per hour (48-80 kilometers per hour) threaten to blast hikers off the trail, made slippery by the thick fog.

Most visitors make it to Skolio Peak, Olympus's second-highest at 9,548 feet (2,911 meters). The easiest peak to reach, Skolio is conveniently located along the E4 trail. Hikers can travel across Europe, even as far away as Spain, along

CHAPTER 5

Skolio Peak

this well-kept path. Just off the E4 trail at Skala Peak, another short trail climbs to Zeus's throne, Olympus's highest peak, Mytikas. This spur trail—known as Kakoskala, or "Evil Staircase"—is a steep and rocky scramble. Though hikers have to get down on all fours, this is actually the safest trail to the summit. Most injuries and deaths happen between Louki peak and Mytikas, a technically challenging trail where landslides often occur.[3]

    At the summit of Mytikas, hikers find whistling winds and grand views of rocks, sea, and sky. A small flagpole flies a metal flag of Greece near a guestbook, where hikers mark their place in Olympus's history. From atop Zeus's ancient perch, the highest point in Greece, hikers see this ancient land in a whole new light. Warring civilizations—and simple goat herders—have lived and died on this mountain for over ten thousand years. Though its people have changed, it seems that Olympus's brown-gray rocks, dusted with snow and clouds, have held up the blue sky and the sea beyond it forever. For a moment, visitors can feel the ancient, raw, and powerful beauty of Olympus, a place that continues to stand the test of time.

CROSSROADS TO THE MUSES

Many hiking trails, some clearly marked, some dangerously not, crisscross the slopes of Olympus. Another popular and easy route to Olympus's peaks is the Diastavrosi (Crossroads) trail. This trailhead lies just north of Prionia, 9 miles (14 kilometers) from Litochoro. Though this trail is longer—7 miles (11 kilometers) compared to the Prionia–Mytikas distance of about 5.5 miles (9 kilometers)—it follows a smooth route along the Lemos Ridge with views of the Aegean Sea, Thessaloniki, and the Macedonian Plain. On very clear days, you can even see Mount Athos.

The Diastavrosi trail is the only path that leads to the Plateau of the Muses, a colorful field of wildflowers and butterflies under the Stefani, Toumba, and Profitis Ilias peaks. The Hellenic Hiking Association maintains the Apostolidis Refuge along this trail, the highest refuge on the mountain at 8,858 feet (2,700 meters). Enjoy fantastic sunrise views from your bed before you set out to hike to the nearby Profitis Ilias Peak.

The Apostolidis Refuge

CHAPTER NOTES

Chapter 1. Climbing the Mountain of Myth

1. Burton A. Falk, "Mount Olympus (Greece): In High Places," The Sierra Club: *Mountaineers,* p. 189. http://angeles.sierraclub.org/sps/archives/sps00546.htm

2. *Let's Go Greece*, ed. Meghan C. Joyce and Jake A. Foley (New York: St. Martin's Press, 2008), p. 288.

3. "British Climber Dies on Mount Olympus," *The Telegraph,* September 4, 2009, http://www.telegraph.co.uk/news/worldnews/europe/greece/6137474/British-climber-dies-on-Mount-Olympus.html

4. Edwin Bernbaum, Sacred Mountains of the World (Berkeley: University of California Press, 1997), p. 108.

Chapter 2. Geography and Environment

1. United States Geological Survey, "Tectonic Summary of Greece," n.d., http://earthquake.usgs.gov/earthquakes/world/greece/tectonic_summary.php

2. *Fodor's Greece,* ed. Robert I. C. Fisher (New York: Fodor's Travel, 2010), p. 359.

3. *Let's Go Greece,* ed. Meghan C. Joyce and Jake A. Foley (New York: St. Martin's Press, 2008), p. 288.

4. Management Agency of Olympus National Park: http://www.olympusfd.gr/us/Default.asp

5. Hellenic Ministry of Culture, "The Broader Region of Mount Olympus," United Nations Educational, Scientific, and Cultural Organization, January 30, 2001, http://whc.unesco.org/en/tentativelists/1790/

6. Arne Strid, Mountain Flora of Greece (Cambridge, UK: Cambridge University Press, 1986), p. xxv.

Chapter 3. History

1. Elaine Thomopoulos, *The History of Greece* (Santa Barbara, CA: Greenwood, 2012), p. 21.

2. Artemis Leontis, *Culture and Customs of Greece* (Westport, CT: Greenwood Press, 2009), p. xv.

CHAPTER NOTES

3. "The Odyssey of the Greek Spirit," *The New York Times,* August 22, 1920; http://select.nytimes.com/gst/abstract.html?res=F5061EF73D5E10728DDDAB0A94D0405B808EF1D3

4. Lord George Gordon Byron, *The Works of Lord Byron,* Vol. 3 (London: John Murray, 1900), p. 20.

5. Elaine Thomopoulos, *The History of Greece* (Santa Barbara, CA: Greenwood, 2012), p. 70.

Chapter 4. The Culture of the Mountains

1. United States Central Intelligence Agency, "Greece," *The World Factbook,* August 29, 2012, https://www.cia.gov/library/publications/the-world-factbook/geos/gr.html

2. Artemis Leontis, *Culture and Customs of Greece* (Westport, CT: Greenwood Press, 2009), p. 102.

3. Associated Press, "Modern Pagans Worship Illegally in Athens," *Sydney Morning Herald*, January 22, 2007.

4. Leontis, p. 64.

Chapter 5. A Trip to Mount Olympus

1. Joanna Kakassis, "Summit of the Gods," *The Boston Globe,* July 17, 2005.

2. Caroline Alexander, "Climbing to the Gods," in *Travelers' Tales: Greece,* ed. Larry Habegger, Sean O'Reilly, and Brian Alexander (San Francisco: Travelers' Tales, 2003), p. 132.

3. Experience Outdoor Activities: "All U Need to Know About Mount Olympus," http://www.experience.gr/mt_olympus/

FURTHER READING

Books

Church, Alfred J. *The Iliad for Boys and Girls.* Chapel Hill, NC: Yesterday's Classics, 2006.

——. *The Odyssey for Boys and Girls.* Chapel Hill, NC: Yesterday's Classics, 2006.

D'Aulaire, Ingri, and Edgar Parin d'Aulaire. *D'Aulaires' Book of Greek Myths.* New York: Delacorte Books for Young Readers, 1992.

Green, Jen. *National Geographic Countries of the World: Greece.* Washington, DC: National Geographic, 2009.

Heinrichs, Ann. *Greece: Enchantment of the World.* New York: Scholastic, 2012.

Pearson, Anne. *Eyewitness: Ancient Greece.* London: Dorling Kindersley Publishers, 2007.

Riordan, Rick. Percy Jackson and the Olympians (series). New York: Disney-Hyperion, 2005–2009.

Steele, Phillip. *Navigators: Ancient Greece.* New York: Kingfisher Books, 2011.

WORKS CONSULTED

Alexander, Caroline. "Climbing to the Gods." *Travelers' Tales: Greece.* Ed. Larry Habegger, Sean O'Reilly, and Brian Alexander. San Francisco: Travelers' Tales, 2003.

Associated Press. "Modern Pagans Worship Illegally in Athens." *Sydney Morning Herald,* January 22, 2007. http://www.smh.com.au/news/travel/modern-pagans-worship-illegally-in-athens/2007/01/22/1169330798194.html?page=2

Bernbaum, Edwin. *Sacred Mountains of the World.* Berkeley: University of California Press, 1997.

"British Climber Dies on Mount Olympus." *The Telegraph,* September 4, 2009. http://www.telegraph.co.uk/news/worldnews/europe/greece/6137474/British-climber-dies-on-Mount-Olympus.html

Byron, Lord George Gordon. *The Works of Lord Byron.* Vol. 3. London: John Murray, 1900.

Douglas, Ed. *Mountaineers: Great Tales of Bravery and Conquest.* New York: DK Publishing, 2011.

Fodor's Greece. Ed. Robert I. C. Fisher. New York: Fodor's Travel, 2010.

Hellenic Ministry of Culture and Tourism. http://odysseus.culture.gr/index_en.html

Hellenic Ministry of Environment, Energy and Climate Change. "Country Profile: Greece." *National Reporting to the 18th and 19th Sessions of the Commission on Sustainable Development of the United Nations,* 2011. http://www.un.org/esa/dsd/dsd_aofw_ni/ni_pdfs/NationalReports/greece/Greece-CSD18-19_Chapter_II-Mining.pdf

Homer. *The Iliad.* Translated by Richmond Lattimore. Chicago: The University of Chicago Press, 2011.

International Olympic Committee. http://www.olympic.org/ioc

Kakassis, Joanna. "Summit of the Gods." *The Boston Globe,* July 17, 2005. http://www.boston.com/travel/articles/2005/07/17/summit_of_the_gods/?page=1

Leontis, Artemis. *Culture and Customs of Greece.* Westport, CT: Greenwood Press, 2009.

Let's Go Greece. Ed. Meghan C. Joyce and Jake A. Foley. New York: St. Martin's Press, 2008.

"Mount Olympus." *Kilian's Quest,* Episodes 3–5. Salomon Running, http://www.salomonrunning.com/us/tv-channel.html?ch=kilian-quest&s=03

BIBLIOGRAPHY

"The Odyssey of the Greek Spirit." *New York Times,* August 22, 1920.

Olympus Marathon Home Page. http://www.olympus-marathon.com

Olympus National Park Home Page. http://www.olympusfd.gr/us/Default.asp

Roberts, Jennifer T., and Tracy Barrett. *The Ancient Greek World.* Oxford, UK: Oxford University Press, 2004.

Smith, Geoffrey W., R. Damian Nance, and Andrew N. Genes. "Quaternary Glacial History of Mount Olympus, Greece." *Geological Society of America Bulletin,* July 1997, vol. 109, no. 7, pp. 809–824.

Strid, Arne. *Mountain Flora of Greece.* Cambridge, UK: Cambridge University Press, 1986.

Thomopoulos, Elaine. *The History of Greece.* Santa Barbara, CA: Greenwood, 2012.

Zeder, Melina A. "Domestication and Early Agriculture in the Mediterranean Basin: Origins, Diffusion, and Impact." *Proceedings of the National Academy of the Sciences,* vol. 105, No. 33, pp. 11597–11604, August 19, 2008.

On the Internet

Ancient Greece
　　http://www.ancientgreece.com/s/Main_Page/

Kilian's Quest, "Mount Olympus" (Season 3, Episodes 3–5)
　　http://www.salomonrunning.com/us/tv-channel.html?ch=kilian-quest

Olympus Climbing
　　https://www.olympus-climbing.gr/

Olympus National Park
　　http://www.olympusfd.gr/us/

Sacred Sites: Mount Olympus
　　http://sacredsites.com/europe/greece/mt_olympus.html

Shutterstock.com Photo Credits: page 5 *town and mountain*, Ion Sebastian; **page 6** *Zeus Temple*, Wagner Santos de Almeida; **page 8** *runner*, Theastock; **page 11** *monastery*, Cristian M Balate; **page 17** *Mytikas*, A.Pushkin; **page 19** *castle sunset*, johzio; **page 27** *town*, ecstk22; **page 29** *statues*, Gilmanshin; **page 31** *Stoa of Attalos*, lovelypeace; **page 34** *church*, Krasimir Lulchev; **page 35** *potato truck*, Alexandros Michailidis; **page 37** *mountain view*, Lev Paraskevopoulos; **page 40** *mountain peak*, dinosmichail; all other sourced images licensed under Creative Commons.

GLOSSARY

city-state—A city and its surrounding area run by an independent government.

diaspora—A group of people who have migrated and scattered away from their homeland.

feta—A soft cheese made from the milk of sheep or goats.

frescoes—Murals painted on fresh plaster, so that the artwork becomes a permanent part of the wall.

Hellenism—Devotion to or imitation of Greek culture or art.

Hellenophilia—Love of Greek culture and language.

herbaceous—A plant that has leaves and stems that die down to the soil level at the end of a growing season.

prominence—The part of a mountain visible above the surrounding foothills.

tectonic plate—A piece of the Earth's crust that moves slowly and interacts with other crust pieces.

tsunami—An extremely large wave or group of waves generated by an earthquake below the ocean's surface.

Goats are natural climbers on the mountain.

INDEX

Aegean Sea 9, 12, 13, 41
Alexander the Great 23
Athens 12, 21, 22, 23, 24, 27, 30, 31, 36, 38
Athos, Mount 25, 41
Balkan Peninsula 7, 8, 12, 14, 16, 24, 25, 27
Baud-Bovy, Daniel 6, 33
Boissonnas, Frédéric 6, 33
Byron, Lord George 26
Byzantine Empire 24, 25
Constantine, Emperor 24
Constantinople 24
Crete 18, 20
diaspora 35, 46
Dion 4, 6, 22
Dionysios, St. 16, 38
Feraios, Rigas 25, 26
Germanic tribes 25
Greece
    ancient history 18, 20–25
    culture 30, 32, 34
    economy 35
    folk music 34
    food 30, 39
    Golden Age of 22
    mineral resources 13–14, 18
    spoken language 24, 32
    sports 20, 34
Greek Orthodox Church 32, 34
Hellenism 26, 46
Hesiod 23
Homer 21, 23, 28
Islam 25, 32
Italy 22, 27
Jornet, Kilian 33
Kakalos, Christos 6–7, 33
Linear A 20, 32
Litochoro 5, 6, 7, 33, 36, 38, 41
Macedonia
    ancient 8, 21, 22
    modern 13, 27, 33, 41

maquis 15
Megali Idea 27
Mehmet IV 6
Metaxas, Ioannis 14, 27
Meteora monasteries 11, 25
Minoan civilization 18, 20, 21, 28
Musala 7
Muses 22, 41
Mycenaeans 8, 20–21, 28
mythology 4, 6, 8, 9, 20–21, 28–29
Olympus Range 13
Olympus Mons 9
Olympus, Mount
    compared to world mountains 7
    geology 10, 12, 13
    origin of name 9, 33
    peaks 4, 6, 7, 8, 9, 12, 13, 14, 17, 33, 36, 38–40, 41
    plant life 14–16, 37
    refuges 38–39, 41
    religious importance 4–6, 20–22
    trails 7, 8, 13, 33, 36, 38–40, 41
    weather 4, 8, 13, 14, 16, 39–40
    wildlife 14–16, 37
Olympus National Park 36, 37
Ottoman Empire 8, 25–26, 32
pagans 32
panigyri 34
Peloponnese 9, 13, 21, 22, 26
Philip II 14, 23
Pindus Range 12–13, 25
Prionia 38, 41
Roman Empire 24, 28–29, 32
Sparta 21–23
Theodosius 32
Thermaic Gulf 4, 13, 14, 16, 38
Thessaloniki 25, 33, 35, 36, 41
Thessaly 13, 21, 22, 26, 27, 33, 36
World War II 27, 38
Zeus 4, 6, 13, 17, 22, 28, 40

ABOUT THE AUTHOR

When Claire O'Neal was nine years old, she discovered the magic of Greek mythology in her school library. Reading these fascinating fairy tales transported her into a lifelong journey of weaving her own stories. To date, O'Neal has written over two dozen books for children. She also holds degrees in English and biology from Indiana University, and a Ph.D. in chemistry from the University of Washington. O'Neal loves to travel, and internationally has visited the UK and New Zealand. She lives in Delaware with her husband and two young sons, where together they dream up their next globetrotting adventures.